MEMPHIS GRIZZLIES

ELLIOTT SMITH

Apex is distributed by North Star Editions:
sales@northstareditions.com | 888-417-0195

Produced for Apex by Red Line Editorial.

Photographs ©: Brandon Dill/AP Images, cover, 1, 47, 57; Brennan Asplen/Getty Images Sport/Getty Images, 4–5; Marta Lavandier/AP Images, 6–7, 58–59; Jonathan Daniel/Allsport/Getty Images Sport/Getty Images, 8–9; Brian Bahr/Allsport/Getty Images Sport/Getty Images, 10–11; Greg Campbell/AP Images, 12–13; Doug Pensinger/Getty Images Sport/Getty Images, 14–15; Ronald Martinez/Getty Images Sport/Getty Images, 16–17, 40–41; Lisa Blumenfeld/Getty Images Sport/Getty Images, 19, 24–25; Chuck Stoody/AP Images, 20–21; Michael Caulfield/AP Images, 22–23; Chris Graythen/Getty Images Sport/Getty Images, 26–27, 30–31; Doug Benc/Getty Images Sport/Getty Images, 28–29; Lance Murphey/AP Images, 32–33; Justin Ford/Getty Images Sport/Getty Images, 34–35, 42–43; Danny Johnston/AP Images, 37; Bob Levey/Getty Images Sport/Getty Images, 38–39; Tim Warner/Getty Images Sport/Getty Images, 44–45; Shutterstock Images, 48–49, 50–51; Christian Petersen/Getty Images Sport/Getty Images, 52–53; Thearon W. Henderson/Getty Images Sport/Getty Images, 54–55

Library of Congress Control Number: 2025943840

ISBN
979-8-89250-907-7 (hardcover)
979-8-89250-938-1 (paperback)
979-8-89824-014-1 (ebook pdf)
979-8-89250-969-5 (hosted ebook)

Printed in the United States of America
Mankato, MN
012026

NOTE TO PARENTS AND EDUCATORS

Apex books are designed to build literacy skills in striving readers. Exciting, high-interest content attracts and holds readers' attention. The text is carefully

TABLE OF CONTENTS

CHAPTER 1

AT THE BUZZER

The Memphis Grizzlies were locked in a battle with the Miami Heat. The teams took turns trading the lead. Time was running out. The score was tied 108–108. The Grizzlies had one final chance to win.

Desmond Bane (22) drives to the hoop during an April 2025 game against the Miami Heat.

Ja Morant dribbled the ball at half-court. He drove into the lane. Then he faded back. A Heat defender jumped up. Morant floated a shot to the basket. It bounced on the rim and fell in. The buzzer sounded. Memphis won!

FEEL THE BEAT

Memphis has its own drum section. The Grizzline gets fans hyped up through music. The group performs in front of the arena before games. The Grizzline also brings the noise during timeouts.

Ja Morant shoots the winning basket in an April 2025 game against the Heat.

CHAPTER 2

EARLY HISTORY

In 1995, the National Basketball Association (NBA) gave a team to Vancouver, British Columbia. Grizzly bears are native to the area. That's why the team was named the Grizzlies. But they struggled for most of their time in Canada.

Greg Anthony was one of the Vancouver Grizzlies' top players during the team's first two seasons.

The Grizzlies had serious money problems. So, the team was sold in 2000. The new owner promised to keep the team in Vancouver. But after the 2000–01 season, he moved the team. The Grizzlies went to Memphis, Tennessee.

NAME GAME

There are no grizzly bears in Tennessee. Many people thought the team would change its name after it moved. But fans in Memphis loved "Grizzlies." It was the same name as an old Memphis football team.

Stromile Swift played for the Grizzlies in both Vancouver and Memphis.

Grizzlies owner Michael Heisley (left) announces the hiring of Jerry West (right).

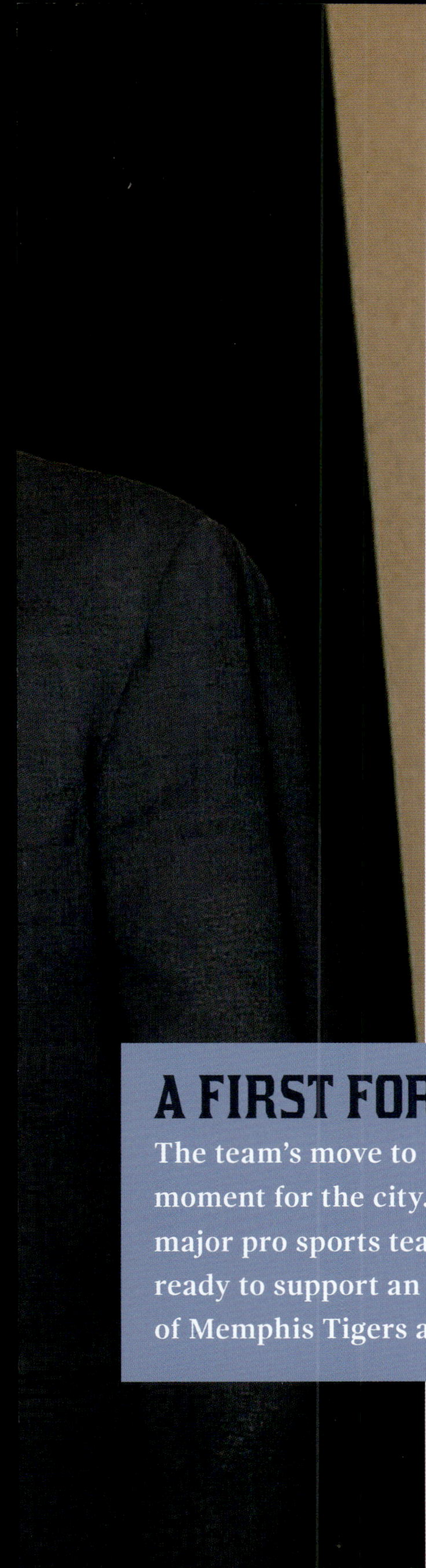

Entering the 2002–03 season, the Grizzlies' best record had been 23–59. It was time for a big change. The Grizzlies hired Jerry West. He became the team's general manager. West was a Los Angeles Lakers legend. He had won one NBA title as a player and six as a general manager.

A FIRST FOR MEMPHIS

The team's move to Memphis was a big moment for the city. They became the first major pro sports team in town. Memphis was ready to support an NBA team. The University of Memphis Tigers already had many fans.

The Grizzlies started off slowly in 2002–03. They were winless in their first eight games. West turned to Hubie Brown for help. Brown was a veteran coach. But he was working as a TV announcer. Brown took the job with Memphis. He provided a breath of fresh air. The players loved him. The Grizzlies didn't have a winning record that season. But they were moving in the right direction.

Hubie Brown won Coach of the Year honors in the 2003–04 season.

Pau Gasol (16) drives to the basket during the Grizzlies' first playoff series in 2004.

The Grizzlies broke through in the 2003–04 season. A young, hungry team went 50–32. That was the best record by far in team history. The Grizzlies reached the playoffs for the first time. After that season, Memphis kept rolling. The Grizzlies made the playoffs two more years in a row.

GROWL TOWELS

In 2004, the Grizzlies passed out towels to fans before playoff games. The "Growl Towels" became a tradition. They often feature popular slogans. Supporters still love collecting them.

PAU GASOL

The Grizzlies picked up Pau Gasol in 2001. The rookie Spaniard stood seven feet (213 cm) tall. And he certainly used his size. He led Memphis in blocks nearly every season he played there. However, Gasol didn't bully his way to the hoop. Instead, he played basketball with grace and a polished technique. In 2002, he became the first non-American NBA player to win the Rookie of the Year Award.

Gasol improved from there. He lifted the Grizzlies to their first playoff appearance in 2004. And in 2006, Gasol became the team's first-ever All-Star.

PAU GASOL SCORED 8,966 POINTS WITH THE GRIZZLIES.

MEMPHIS
16

CHAPTER 3

LEGENDS

Bryant Reeves was the first draft pick in team history. Injuries limited his career to six seasons. But they were all with the Grizzlies. The burly center was a bruiser. He averaged 12.5 points per game.

Bryant Reeves made the All-Rookie Team in the 1995–96 season.

The Grizzlies drafted Shareef Abdur-Rahim in 1996. He was the third overall pick that year. The forward became the team's first true star. Abdur-Rahim provided steady scoring. He averaged more than 20 points per game over five seasons.

REBOUNDS AND DUNKS

Stromile Swift was another top draft pick. The Grizzlies chose him with the second overall pick in the 2000 draft. Swift was a fierce rebounder. And fans loved his huge dunks.

Shareef Abdur-Rahim scored 1,829 points in the 1997–98 season. As of 2025, that remained a Grizzlies record.

Shane Battier drives during a 2005 game against the Los Angeles Lakers.

The Grizzlies drafted Shane Battier in 2001. He started his career when the team moved to Memphis. Battier was a defensive whiz. He used smarts and hustle to draw fouls. The Grizzlies traded Battier after five seasons. But he came back in 2011.

GAME-WINNER

Shane Battier played for the Grizzlies during their first three playoff runs. However, Memphis was swept each time. The team returned to the playoffs in 2011. Battier was back, too. He hit a game-winning three-pointer in Game 1. That gave the Grizzlies their first-ever playoff win.

Rudy Gay joined the Grizzlies as a rookie in 2006. The forward showed no rookie nerves. The next season, Gay led the team in scoring. He helped lead Memphis back to the playoffs in 2011.

SIXTH MAN

Mike Miller joined Memphis in 2003. He became a key bench player. In 2006, he won the NBA's Sixth Man of the Year Award. Miller became known for his long-range buckets. In January 2007, he hit nine three-pointers in a game. He did it again in February.

Rudy Gay averaged 17.9 points per game with Memphis.

CHAPTER 4

RECENT HISTORY

The Grizzlies went 22–60 in the 2006–07 season. After that, Jerry West stepped down as the team's general manager. Memphis traded Pau Gasol in the middle of the next season. The team struggled to rebuild.

Pau Gasol's best scoring season came in 2006–07. He averaged 20.8 points per game.

Mike Conley (11) defends a shot during a 2010 game against New Orleans.

In 2009, the Grizzlies picked up forward Zach Randolph. And point guard Mike Conley became a full-time starter. Conley helped the Grizzlies play a tough defensive style. These teams were nicknamed the "Grit and Grind" Grizzlies. They didn't have big stars. But they became fan favorites.

TRADING BROTHERS

The Grizzlies traded Pau Gasol in 2008. In return, they got his younger brother Marc. The move was the first sibling trade in NBA history. Marc became the next face of the Grizzlies.

Zach Randolph (50) scored 31 points in Game 6 to beat the San Antonio Spurs in the 2011 playoffs.

By 2010–11, the Grizzlies had returned to the playoffs. They were the No. 8 seed. But they beat the top-seeded San Antonio Spurs in six games. It was the first time the Grizzlies had won a playoff series. And it was only the fourth time a No. 8 seed had beaten a No. 1.

SOLD!

Businessman Robert Pera bought the Grizzlies in 2012. The price was about $350 million. Pera pledged to keep the team in Memphis. That relieved Grizzlies fans. Many had feared the team would move.

The Grizzlies went a team-best 56–26 in 2012–13. Then they reached their first conference finals. And in 2017, they made their seventh straight playoffs. The Grizzlies struggled after that. But they drafted Ja Morant in 2019. He helped the team become playoff contenders again.

HEAD OF THE CLASS

Dave Joerger was a longtime Grizzlies assistant. He took over as head coach in 2013. Joerger remained with Memphis until 2016. During that time, he set the team record for best winning percentage.

In 2021–22, the Grizzlies won their division for the first time ever.

PLAYER SPOTLIGHT

ZACH RANDOLPH

Zach Randolph joined the Grizzlies in 2009–10. The forward quickly became a fan favorite. He earned his first All-Star nod that season. Randolph combined his size with agility. That made him a great rebounder. And his intensity fueled the "Grit and Grind" Grizzlies.

Randolph spent eight seasons with Memphis. He averaged nearly 17 points per game. In 2021, Randolph received a big honor. The Grizzlies retired his No. 50 jersey. It was the first retired jersey in team history.

ZACH RANDOLPH LEADS THE GRIZZLIES IN CAREER OFFENSIVE REBOUNDS.

CHAPTER 5

MODERN STARS

Marc Gasol became a great leader for Memphis. The center spent 11 seasons with the team. As of 2025, he still led the Grizzlies in several major categories. They included rebounds and blocks.

Marc Gasol had 1,135 blocks with the Grizzlies.

Memphis drafted Mike Conley in 2007. He played a key role in the Grizzlies' turnaround. As of 2025, Conley remained Memphis's leader in points. He also led in assists and steals.

Conley played in Memphis through 2018–19. That was Jaren Jackson Jr.'s first season. The rookie carried on Conley's defensive legacy. Jackson earned Defensive Player of the Year honors in 2023.

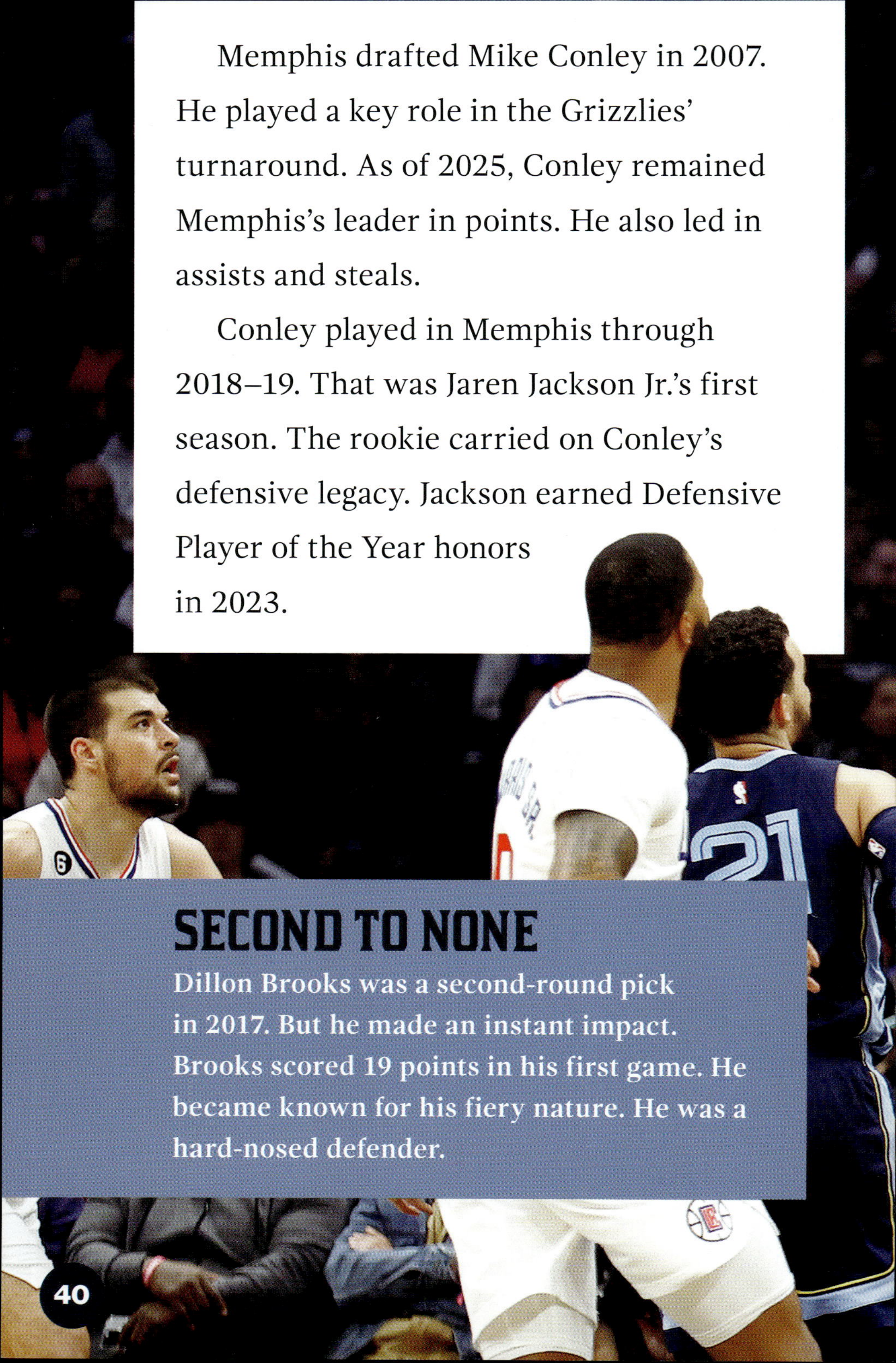

SECOND TO NONE

Dillon Brooks was a second-round pick in 2017. But he made an instant impact. Brooks scored 19 points in his first game. He became known for his fiery nature. He was a hard-nosed defender.

Jaren Jackson Jr. led the NBA in blocks in 2021–22 and 2022–23.

Desmond Bane provided huge scoring for the Grizzlies. He kept it up in the postseason. In the 2023 playoffs, he averaged 23.5 points per game. His scoring increased the next season. In one game, he scored 49 points. That was a career high.

CLUTCH CLARKE

Brandon Clarke shined in the 2022 playoffs. He helped Memphis beat the Minnesota Timberwolves. In Game 6, Clarke racked up 17 points. He grabbed 11 rebounds. He also recorded five assists and three blocks. And he did all of that off the bench.

On March 3, 2025, Desmond Bane (22) recorded his first triple-double.

The Grizzlies drafted Zach Edey in 2024. He became a powerful force in the paint. The center stood seven feet, four inches (224 cm) tall. That made him the tallest active NBA player.

RISING TALENT

Santi Aldama became a Grizzly in 2021. In his first season, he averaged just 4.1 points per game. But Aldama improved his scoring in each of his first four seasons. The forward averaged 12.5 points in 2024–25.

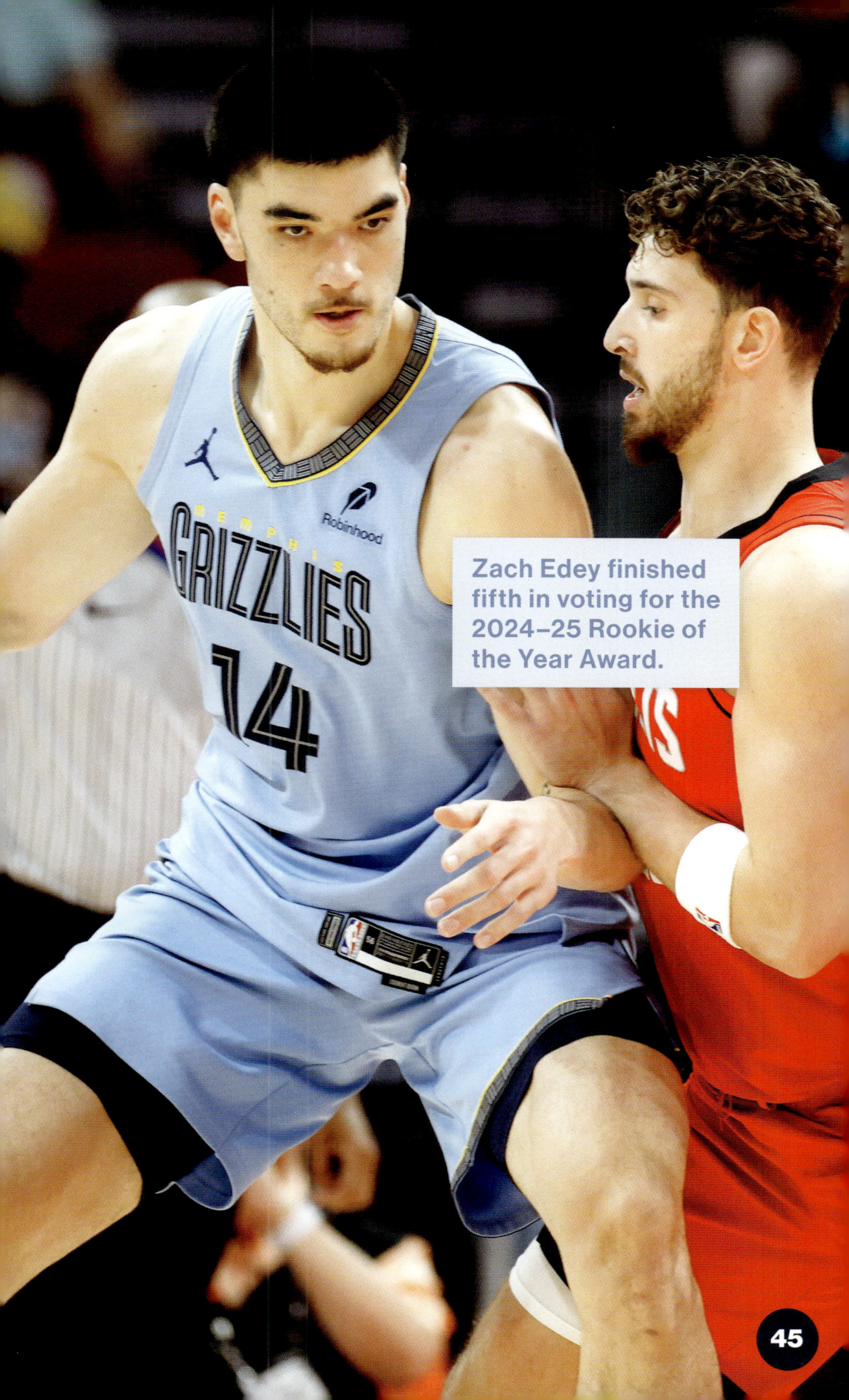

Zach Edey finished fifth in voting for the 2024–25 Rookie of the Year Award.

PLAYER SPOTLIGHT

JA MORANT

Scoring in the paint is often left to the big men. That doesn't apply to Ja Morant. In 2022–23, he led the NBA in points in the paint. He was the first guard to do so in years.

Morant stands only six feet, two inches (188 cm) tall. That's short for an NBA player. But he has explosive speed. He boasts great ball-handling skills. And his control at the rim is elite. Morant cuts through defenses for smooth layups and amazing dunks. He also scores on floaters against the game's best centers.

JA MORANT WON THE ROOKIE OF THE YEAR AWARD IN 2019–20.

FedEx
GRIZZLIES
12

CHAPTER 6

TEAM TRIVIA

At first, Vancouver's team was going to be called the Mounties. But the Royal Canadian Mounted Police complained. That forced the change to the Grizzlies.

The Royal Canadian Mounted Police are the national police of Canada.

The Grizzlies played their first Memphis home games at the Pyramid. The arena was one of the most unusual in sports. It was based on the ancient pyramids in Egypt. The building is one of the largest pyramids in the world.

FULL-COURT BUZZER-BEATER

Memphis had the ball in a 2022 game. Just 0.4 seconds were left before halftime. Grizzlies center Steven Adams heaved an inbounds pass. It traveled 92 feet (28 m) downcourt. Ja Morant caught the ball in midair. He shot it before he landed. The ball fell through the net at the buzzer. The pass was the longest assist in NBA history.

The Grizzlies played at the Pyramid for three seasons.

Grizz thrills fans with slam dunks during timeouts.

Grizz is the team's high-flying mascot. The bear has been with the team since 1995. In 2007, the performer who played Grizz became sick. So, other NBA mascots visited the Grizzlies' arena. They helped fire up fans. The performer recovered and returned in 2008. In 2011, Grizz won Mascot of the Year.

CITY CONNECT

The Grizzlies' jerseys are light blue and navy blue. They also feature yellow and gray. Memphis has worn other jerseys, too. They often reflect the city's culture. Some jerseys honored the city's music history. Others noted its important place in civil rights history.

The Grizzlies haven't been around as long as most NBA teams. But they've started adding Hall of Famers to their ranks. Pau Gasol joined the Hall of Fame in 2023. He was the first Hall of Fame player who'd spent at least one season as a Grizzly. Vince Carter became the second in 2024.

END OF AN ERA

Point Guard Mike Bibby ended his NBA career in 2012. He had played for the Grizzlies from 1998 to 2001. The team was still in Vancouver then. Bibby was the last active player who'd played for Vancouver.

Vince Carter shoots a jumper during a 2017 game.

TEAM RECORDS

All-Time Points: 11,733
Mike Conley (2007–19)

All-Time Assists: 4,509
Mike Conley (2007–19)

All-Time Rebounds: 5,942
Marc Gasol (2008–19)

All-Time Steals: 1,161
Mike Conley (2007–19)

All-Time Blocks: 1,135
Marc Gasol (2008–19)

All-Time Three-Pointers: 1,086
Mike Conley (2007–19)

All-Time Triple-Doubles: 12
Ja Morant (2019–)

All-Time Points Per Game: 22.6
Ja Morant (2019–)

All-Time Games Played: 788
Mike Conley (2007–19)

All-Time Coaching Wins: 250
Taylor Jenkins (2019–25)

All statistics are accurate through the 2024–25 season.

TIMELINE

1995
The Grizzlies begin playing in Vancouver, British Columbia.

2001
The Grizzlies move to Memphis, Tennessee.

2004
Memphis makes the playoffs for the first time in team history.

2008
Pau Gasol is traded to the Los Angeles Lakers. The Grizzlies get his brother Marc in return.

2010
Mike Conley helps lead the "Grit and Grind" Grizzlies.

2011

Memphis wins a playoff game and a playoff series for the first time.

2012

Robert Pera buys the Grizzlies for $350 million. He vows to keep team in Memphis.

2013

The Grizzlies have a team-record 56–26 season and reach the conference finals.

2019

Memphis selects Ja Morant with the second pick in the draft. Morant wins Rookie of the Year.

2025

The Grizzlies make the playoffs for the 14th time in team history.

COMPREHENSION QUESTIONS

Write your answers on a separate piece of paper.

1. Write a paragraph that explains the main ideas of Chapter 4.

2. Who do you think was the greatest player in Grizzlies history? Why?

3. Who was the Grizzlies' first All-Star?

   A. Marc Gasol
   B. Pau Gasol
   C. Zach Randolph

4. Why is scoring in the paint often left to the big men?

   A. Big players can shoot over defenders.
   B. Big players usually have excellent quickness.
   C. Big players focus on scoring three-pointers.

5. What does **tradition** mean in this book?

In 2004, the Grizzlies passed out towels to fans before playoff games. The "Growl Towels" became a ***tradition****. They often feature popular slogans. Supporters still love collecting them.*

- **A.** a one-time event that is not popular
- **B.** a way of doing something over many years
- **C.** a difficult job that nobody wants to do

6. What does **heaved** mean in this book?

Grizzlies center Steven Adams ***heaved*** *an inbounds pass. It traveled 92 feet (28 m) downcourt. Ja Morant caught the ball in midair.*

- **A.** rebounded
- **B.** blocked
- **C.** threw

Answer key on page 64.

GLOSSARY

assists
Passes that lead directly to baskets.

conference
A group of teams that make up part of a sports league.

draft
A system that lets teams select new players coming into the league.

mascot
A figure that is the symbol of a sports team.

paint
The area between the basket and the free-throw line.

playoffs
A set of games played after the regular season to decide which team is the champion.

retired
Honored a player by deciding that his or her jersey number may not be worn by another player.

rookie
An athlete in his or her first year as a professional player.

seed
A team's ranking heading into a tournament.

technique
The way a person performs certain movements, usually to do a specific job.

veteran
A person who has been doing his or her job for a long time and has a lot of experience.

TO LEARN MORE

BOOKS

Clarke, David J. *Memphis Grizzlies All-Time Greats*. Press Box Books, 2024.

Grack, Rachel A. *Everything NBA*. Bellwether Media, 2026.

Whiting, Jim. *The Story of the Memphis Grizzlies*. Creative Education, 2023.

ONLINE RESOURCES

Visit **www.apexeditions.com** to find links and resources related to this title.

ABOUT THE AUTHOR

Elliott Smith is a writer in the Washington, DC, area. As a reporter, he covered sports from high school to the pros. As an author, he's written more than 90 books, both fiction and nonfiction, about sports and history.

INDEX

ANSWER KEY:

1. Answers will vary; 2. Answers will vary; 3. B; 4. A; 5. B; 6. C